An April Song

Copyright © 2017 Read Books Ltd.
This book is copyright and may not be
reproduced or copied in any way without
the express permission of the publisher in writing

British Library Cataloguing-in-Publication Data
A catalogue record for this book is available from the
British Library

An April Song

NEW POEMS

by

CHARLES HANSON TOWNE

By *Charles Hanson Towne*

THE QUIET SINGER AND OTHER POEMS
MANHATTAN, A POEM
YOUTH, AND OTHER POEMS
BEYOND THE STARS, AND OTHER POEMS
TODAY AND TOMORROW, AND OTHER POEMS
LOAFING DOWN LONG ISLAND
THIS NEW YORK OF MINE
GOOD OLD YESTERDAY
TINSEL
THE CHAIN
AN APRIL SONG, NEW POEMS

Charles Hanson Towne

Charles Hanson Towne was born in 1877; an author, poet, editor and popular celebrity, he spent most of his life in New York. Towne spent his early life in Kentucky however, moving to the city with his family at the age of three. He began his literary career remarkably early - at the age of eleven when he became the 'publisher' of the *Unique Monthly*, a children's magazine written by and for Towne and his friends. His first real job came with a position as editorial assistant at *Cosmopolitan* (originally a family magazine, and a literary journal during Towne's era). In 1901, Towne moved up the career ladder to *Smart Set*, a publication squarely aimed at sophisticated urban clients. He was remarkably successful with this company, and was appointed overall editor in 1904 - a trend which continued for the remainder of his career.

Towne also wrote many of his own much celebrated poems, plays, essays and novels - on various subjects surrounding life in New York City. Through this oeuvre, he quickly became known as the 'quintessential New Yorker', carrying on with his editorial duties at magazines such as *Delineator, Designer, McClure's and Harper's Bazaar*. Some of Towne's best known poems include: *Beyond the Stars,* a work which invites the reader not to fear death, but revel in its glory, *Around the Corner,* another poem which speaks of friendship and loss - yet hopes for 'tomorrow', and *Manhattan: A Poem,* speaking of his love of the great American city.

For almost the entire 1930s, Towne wrote a personal and literary column for the *New York American,* as well as making use of his fame in the poetry world, by teaching a poetry course at Columbia University. Towne was never a man to settle down though, and in 1940, joined the touring company of the Broadway show, *Life with Father.* His exploits have all been documented for posterity with his autobiography, *So Far, So Good.* Towne died in 1949, at the age of seventy-two. He left behind a vast amount of writing, still much renowned today.

A Brief History of Poetry

'Poetry' as an art form, has an incredibly long history – it may even predate literacy and the written word. At its purest, poetry is simply a form of communication using aesthetic and rhythmic qualities of language to evoke meanings over and above the ostensible and everyday meaning of words. The earliest poetry is believed to have been recited or sung; employed as a way of remembering oral history, genealogy, and law.

Many scholars, particularly those researching the Homeric tradition and the oral epics of the Balkans, suggest that early writing shows clear traces of older oral traditions, including the use of repeated phrases as building blocks in larger poetic units. A rhythmic and repetitious form would make a long story easier to remember and retell, before writing was available as an *aide-memoire*. Thus many ancient works, from the Vedas (1700 - 1200 BCE) to the *Odyssey* (800 - 675 BCE), appear to have been composed in poetic form to aid memorization and oral transmission. Poetry appears among the earliest records of most literate cultures, with poetic fragments found on early monoliths, runestones and stelae.

The oldest surviving speculative fiction poem is the *Tale of the Shipwrecked Sailor*, written in *Hieratic* and ascribed a date around 2500 BCE. Other sources ascribe the earliest written poetry to the *Epic of Gilgamesh* written in *cuneiform*; however, it is most likely that *The Tale of the Shipwrecked Sailor* predates *Gilgamesh* by half a millennium. The oldest epic poetry besides the *Epic of Gilgamesh* are the Greek epics *Iliad* and *Odyssey*, and the Indian Sanskrit epics *Ramayana and Mahabharata*.

In the Western poetic tradition, meters are customarily grouped according to a characteristic 'metrical foot' and the number of feet per line. The number of metrical feet in a line are described using Greek terminology: tetrameter for four feet and hexameter for six feet, for example. Thus, 'iambic pentameter' is a meter comprising five feet per line, in which the predominant kind of foot is the 'iamb'. This metric system originated in ancient Greek poetry, and was used by poets such as Pindar and Sappho, and by the great tragedians of Athens. Similarly, 'dactylic hexameter', comprises six feet per line, of which the dominant kind of foot is the 'dactyl'. Dactylic hexameter was the traditional meter of Greek epic poetry, the earliest extant examples of which are the works of Homer and Hesiod. Iambic pentameter and dactylic hexameter were later used by a number of poets, including William Shakespeare and Henry Wadsworth Longfellow.

Different traditions and genres of poetry tend to use different meters, ranging from the Shakespearean iambic pentameter and the Homeric dactylic hexameter to the anapestic tetrameter used in many nursery rhymes. Rhyme, alliteration, assonance and consonance are ways of creating repetitive patterns of sound. They may be used as an independent structural element in a poem, to reinforce rhythmic patterns, or as an ornamental element. They can also carry a meaning separate from the repetitive sound patterns created. For example, Chaucer used heavy alliteration to mock Old English verse and to paint a character as archaic. Poetry can also rely on a heavy visual aspect, often underappreciated. Even before the advent of printing, the visual appearance of poetry often added meaning or depth. In Arabic, Hebrew, Chinese, and much modernist poetry, the visual presentation of finely calligraphed poems has played an important part in the overall effect.

Ancient thinkers sought to determine what makes poetry distinctive as a form and what distinguishes good poetry from bad, resulting in the development of 'poetics', or the study of the aesthetics of poetry. Some ancient societies, such as the Chinese through the *Classic of History*, one of the 'Five Classics', developed canons of poetic works that had ritual as well as aesthetic importance. More recently, thinkers have struggled to find a definition that could encompass formal differences as great as those between Chaucer's *The Canterbury Tales* and Matsuo Bashō's *Oku no Hosomichi*, as well as differences in context that span from the religious poetry of the Tanakh, to love poetry, to rap.

Classical thinkers employed classification as a way to define and assess the quality of poetry. Notably, the existing fragments of Aristotle's *Poetics* describe three genres of poetry – the epic, the comic, and the tragic – and develop rules to distinguish the highest-quality poetry in each genre, based on the underlying purposes of the genre. Aristotle's work was influential throughout the Middle East during the Islamic Golden Age, as well as in Europe during the Renaissance. Later poets and aestheticians often distinguished poetry from, and defined it in opposition to prose, which was generally understood as writing with a proclivity to logical explication and a linear narrative structure.

This does not imply that poetry is illogical or lacks narration, but rather that poetry is an attempt to render the beautiful or sublime without the burden of engaging the logical or narrative thought process. English Romantic poet John Keats termed this escape from logic 'Negative Capability'. This 'romantic' approach views form as a key element of successful poetry because form is abstract and distinct from the underlying notional logic. This approach remained influential into the twentieth century. During this period, there was also substantially more interaction among the various poetic traditions, in part due to the spread of European colonialism and the attendant rise in global trade. In addition to this, there was a boom in translation during the Romantic period, when numerous ancient works were rediscovered.

The rejection of traditional forms and structures for poetry that began in the first half of the twentieth century coincided with a questioning of the purpose and meaning of traditional definitions of poetry – and of distinctions between poetry and prose, particularly given examples of poetic prose and prosaic poetry. Numerous modernist poets have written in non-traditional forms or in what traditionally would have been considered prose, although their writing was generally infused with poetic diction and often with rhythm and tone established by non-metrical means. Recently, postmodernism has come to convey more completely prose and poetry as distinct entities, and also among genres of poetry, as having meaning only as cultural artefacts. Postmodernism goes beyond modernism's emphasis on the creative role of the poet, to emphasize the role of the reader of a text (Hermeneutics), and to highlight the complex cultural web within which a poem is read.

Today, throughout the world, poetry often incorporates poetic form and diction from other cultures and from the past, further confounding attempts at definition and classification that were once sensible within a tradition such as the Western canon. There are an astounding array of 'types' of poetry, for instance historical epics, poetry for liturgical purposes (hymns, psalms, suras and hadiths), popular music, elegies, romance and tragedies, political invective, and light hearted nursery or nonsense rhymes. The use of verse to transmit cultural information continues in the present, and the poetic arts show no signs of abating – in fact, their development continues apace. It is hoped that the current reader enjoys this book on the subject.

TO THE BEAUTIFUL MEMORY OF

EMILY STEVENS

CONTENTS

THE BALLAD OF BROTHER ANSELM	3
LONG SILENT	8
EASTER	9
PARTING AT A STATION	10
LILACS	11
CITIES	12
SNOW ON HER HAIR	13
THE OLD MIRACLE	14
WE HAVE TURNED AGAIN HOME	15
GENIUS	16
"IF LIFE WERE ONLY LOVE"	18
THE TERRORISTS	19
IN AUTUMN	20
BALLADE OF RETURN	21
SUDDENLY OLD	23

AUTUMN GOING	24
AN APRIL SONG	26
KERRY	27
FUGITIVE	29
ALONE WITH OUR BOOKS	30
THE DEATHLESS TALE	33
SLOWLY	35
JAPANESE MAIDENHAIR TREES	36
THE MOON AT THE END OF THE STREET	37
CHOICE	39
A CHARITY DANCE	40
ON RECEIVING A FLORIST'S BILL	42
BLIND IN THE CITY	43
SIX LITTLE IVORY ELEPHANTS	44
WHEN WE WERE POOR IN PARIS	45
DEAD TREE	47
ASSUNTA'S ROSE	48
OLD DRY-AS-DUST	51

An April Song

The Ballad of Brother Anselm
(An Old Legend)

Now it was Brother Anselm
    Who, when young April came,
Stood at the monastery door,
    And watched the crocus flame;
Then crossed himself and whispered, "Lord,
    Lord, now I bless Thy name."

For beauty seethed across the earth:
    White foam trailed through the skies,
A benediction touched the land,
    And opened paradise.
"Now God be praised!" . . . The good monk raised
    His young, astonished eyes.

He fared him forth into the fields,
    And long the path he trod.
He felt the lure of growing things,
    He smelt the sweet green sod;
And like a lonely cedar tree,
    He was alone with God.

White hyacinths, forget-me-nots
    And lilies pale as pearls—

All these he saw, as, dumb with awe,
    He walked where water whirls,
And where the playful Springtime wind
    Lifts up the grass in curls.

Suddenly from the morning skies,
    (His cell had been so dark!)
There dropped a golden coin of sound,
    And Anselm whispered, "Hark!
I never heard a sound more sweet—
    Is it the meadow-lark?"

And he who, prisoned many days
    Through all his youthful years
Had never crossed these blowing fields,
    Looked up with sudden tears.
It was as if the voice of God
    Struck his astounded ears.

Oh, sweet, thrice sweet the silver rain
    Of song that trembled down.
It kissed the petals of the grass,
    It touched the monk's white gown,
And delicately shook the flowers
    Not yet to fulness grown.

He stood, transfixed. Was it a sin
    That, far from his dim cell,
He listened to this flutelike voice
    That trilled its song so well?

Silent he stood close to a wood,
    Lost in the music's spell.

The first lark's song that he had heard!
    In golden showers of sound,
In laughing cataracts of joy
    Its splashing way it found
To the young monk's uplifted heart—
    Then broke upon the ground.

Dazed and amazed Fra Anselm stood.
    Unheard the ancient bell
That summoned him, at twilight dim,
    Back to his lonely cell.
He listened only to that song—
    Celestial miracle.

Day dwindled; yet he listened on,
    Then Time itself stood still.
Forgotten were his years within
    The gray house on the hill.
The lark's pure song had vanquished Wrong,
    And conquered every ill.

How long he stood he never knew
    Till, at pale vesper time,
He knocked on the familiar door
    Beneath the belfry's chime,
And the song of the bird that he had heard
    Was but a vanished rhyme.

"Who knocks?" a strange voice came to him
    Through the sweet afternoon.
" 'Tis Brother Anselm," answered he;
    "Open, and open soon,
For I would say my vesper prayers
    Before the rise o' the moon."

"Anselm?" the other, opening, said;
    "And who art thou, pale brother?"
"I am Fra Anselm," answered he,
    "Fra Anselm, and no other.
Come, let me in. I bear no sin
    Greater than any other."

There was a whisper in the court
    Beyond the oaken door.
Cowled heads were bent in disassent.
    "Who is he?" o'er and o'er
Went the strange word which Anselm heard,
    And his young heart grew sore.

Great tomes were brought. His name was sought;
    Pale fingers traced each page.
At last, " 'Tis here!" the whisper clear
    Came from one old and sage.
"A Brother Anselm dwelt here once,
    But in a distant age."

An hundred years had passed, as though
    A single hour were flung

Into the tide whereon we glide,
    Be we old or young.
For Anselm, Time was blotted out
    When the lark's song was sung.

An hundred Aprils had gone by,
    And Anselm had been dead
To those within that quiet place
    Where once he used to tread,
Telling his beads for sinners' needs
    When the white dawn grew red.

An hundred Springs had drifted on,
    Whilst Anselm tarried, lost,
Lost in the beauty of that song
    Through days of bitter frost,
Through fiery Autumns of the years,
    And Winter's holocaust.

"Now God be praised!" young Anselm said,
    And strode to his old cell.
The monks, bewildered, watched him go—
    Was this a miracle?
And Anselm, turning, whispered low,
    "Dear brothers, all is well!"

Long Silent

Our Poet had been long silent. He had sung
    In his golden youth, of the moon and the stars,
And the whispering winds, and the light that clung
    In the heavens after evening put up her bars.

Now, after an aching interval, he came
    With a new song from the old heart in his breast.
And over our world there burst a beautiful flame,
    His last song his sweetest song, and his best.

But not of Death was his music, nor of tears.
    He sang of youth and April, and the days of his prime.
For only the old can know the glory of young years,
    And only the old can sing of Once-on-a-time.

Easter

The buds have broken on every bough;
The world is sweet with laughing sun.
The hills are white with promise now—
Spring has begun.

Out of the cold come leaf and grass,
And out of darkness sweeps the light.
Ah! we have watched the winter pass,
With its deep night.

But O, my heart, a gentler Flower
Has lighted earth's enormous room,
And in this bright Aprilian hour
Shattered the tomb.

And every year this Bloom bursts through;
The new-old miracle we see,
And if the lilies of light are true,
Ah! so is **He**!

Parting at a Station

We said good-bye; and then
    The small pane framed your face.
How sweet had been our last long kiss,
    How wild our last embrace!

O strange it was that I
    Who loved you then the more,
Should turn that instant, glad to move
    Through the train's gulf-like door.

I loved you. Yet I loved
    Our separation too. . . .
One hour, and I had given the world
    To be once more with you!

Lilacs

Now, with the first sweet breath of Spring,
The lilacs sway, the lilacs swing;
    And in the moonlight,
    The ghostly moonlight,
I swear I hear the lilacs sing.

Here, where the April trumpets blow,
And the world is white with flowery snow,
    In the gold sunlight,
    The passionate sunlight,
The lilacs nod, and whisper—so.

Before this house of ruin and pain,
In the slow rush of the April rain,
    In the blue darkness,
    The sudden darkness,
The lilacs are ghosts come back again.

Then, with the first wild winds of Spring,
When the world is mad with blossoming,
    In the pale moonlight,
    The haunted moonlight,
I swear I hear the lilacs sing!

Cities

I shall live to see a City built of brass,
    Or perhaps of pure gold, as in Solomon's reign.
One thing I know; one thing I am certain of, alas!
    Always this City shall be built of tears and pain,
    Always of tears and pain.

No matter how old and lovely our City may be;
    No matter how long her wonderful, dreaming years,
Always her children shall suffer unutterably,
    Always for them there shall be pain and tears,
    Always old pain and tears.

For cities, like Tyre, and Dis, and our modern walls,
    Are builded by man; even so into being came Rome.
And thus if Nineveh crumbles, and Carthage falls,
    Our City must sink in the end 'neath the sea or the loam,
    Though it once was our home.

Snow On Her Hair

We walked through the winter dusk, and oh, but she was fair,
My love with the soft white snow upon her raven hair.
We laughed in the falling dark, till we reached our candle's ray;
But the beautiful snow on her hair had gone away.

We sit through the dusk of life, when the last snow falls down,
And white on her lovely brow is this silvery crown.
We had laughed at the fleeting snow, in those years far away,
But this white snow will remain forever and a day.

The Old Miracle

I saw once more, as with new eyes,
    The dream of winter fade and pass,
And earth grow sweet beneath the skies—
    Oh, green ascension of the grass!

Forever old, forever new,
    I saw the larkspur shine again,
And hawthorn break, and violets blue
    Open their eyes after light rain.

The hyacinths held up their hands,
    And apple blossoms starred the trees;
Beauty that no one understands
    Came with her soft spring mysteries.

I said, "My heart will break with bliss—
    Too much pale loveliness I see."
Yet the least joy I feared to miss,
    Or the least bud on yonder tree.

And still I drank the wonder up;
    I could not know my fill thereof.
Who yet has drained the tulip's cup,
    And who has known too much of love?

We Have Turned Again Home

Heart, O my Heart, we have turned again home!
After the desolate wanderings and the search for renown,
We have come back with a sweet assurance,
And the distant towers and turrets are tumbling down.

How forgotten are the dreams that we dreamed in the old
    days,
And how remembered now the little beautiful things.
Long, long we sought the elusive shadows of greatness,
The dangerous baubles and counterfeits of kings.

Now, down the simple highways we return at last.
The scent of the hedge is keen, and the grass, and the loam.
How could we ever have followed our foolish phantoms?—
Heart, O my Heart, we have turned again home!

Genius

Who gave this flame to him
    That burns within his brain?
From heaven's remotest rim
    There came the joy—and pain.

He walks our clamoring streets,
    Unmindful of the crowd;
But ever in him beats
    A rhythm wild and loud.

And often in the night
    He stares at the torn moon,
And darkness is as bright
    As the great eye of noon.

Only his dreams we know.
    We never guess the grief
That wanders to and fro
    Like a blown autumn leaf.

His loneliness we fail
    To understand; the dread
That presses like a nail
    Upon his tortured head.

The awful price he pays
    For this, his gift of song!
The shadows on his days,
    His iron nights, how long!

For, ever in him burns
    A fire that will not cease,
While his hot spirit yearns
    For islands cool with peace.

"If Life Were Only Love"

If life were only love, then life would be
As wearisome as an untroubled sea;
Monotonous as prairies in the sun,
Level and long, which even the gods would shun,
But life is love for only one brief hour.
There is a moment when the perfect flower
Blossoms and breaks, dew-wet and beautiful,
A lily on the clear glass of a pool.
One instant—so it seems!—of rich, high joy;
And then the fates that build, also destroy,
And the white moment passes. Love is gone
As swiftly as the evanescent dawn.
Yet there can be no life without that hour;
And pressed within Life's book, there is a flower.

The Terrorists

I hear the thunder of the sea,
    As though the waves are in revolt—
A splendid, awful anarchy.
    "Tear down the world's last bar and bolt!"
This is the cry the wild sea sings,
As on the shore its weight it flings.

How desperate these legions are!
    Impetuous and ill at ease,
They crowd across the harbor-bar,
    And shout their ancient blasphemies.
"We shall destroy the coastline soon!" . . .
Serene above them floats the moon.

In Autumn

I walked within the autumn woods
    When all the leaves were burnished gold;
I said, "How lovely it will be
    When I too have grown old."

For old folk nod, like trees, and dream
    Bright dreams that never seem to cease.
Their days flow by in a long stream,
    Touched with mysterious peace.

And here the woods were burning up,
    A fire that flamed through the year's night.
They burned with memory of spring's cup
    And youth's long-gone delight.

Old, old and worn these autumn woods;
    Yet there is beauty in such gold.
Ah! to be lonely like the moon,
    And old, as stars are old!

Ballade of Return

How strange it is that we forget
    All beauty does not really go.
The sunlight on a minaret
    Returns with evening's afterglow.
    And always the faint heart should know
After the winter's wind and rain,
    After the ghostly pall of snow,
The birds and bees come back again.

The bitter seasons bring their fret,
    The world may rock with want and woe,
And war's red tumult may beget
    New agony; but even so
    White peace shall follow, honey flow,
And blossoms be where blood has lain.
    Thanks be to heaven, bright buds shall blow,
The birds and bees come back again.

What though today our eyes are wet,
    Because our dreams have vanished? No,
They have not died—not yet, not yet,
    Nor shall their grave be dug below.
    Madness and panic overthrow

The kindled hopes in heart and brain;
    But now, as in the long ago,
The birds and bees come back again.

L'Envoi:

Love, though we vanish, and although
    We seem but wasted chaff and grain,
Music endures, and beauty. Oh,
    The birds and bees come back again!

Suddenly Old

Suddenly she grew old. It was as though
In the late Summer there should come white snow;
As if the afternoon turned swiftly dim,
And darkness touched the sun's receding rim.

And yet, what peace was hers! what beauty now
Rested upon her lips, her eyes, her brow,
As if remembered mornings had returned
And with a sweeter lustre beamed and burned.

Autumn Going

I

Now autumn goes in purple
    And crimson livery.
The year that has been dying
    Will soon be free—be free.
Beyond the gates of sunset
    What loveliness may be!

Oh, not with sorrow passes
    The ancient, leaf-strewn year.
She goes in jubilation,
    Devoid of haunting fear.
How rich are all the hills today,
    When shadows disappear!

II

Thus I must don deep raiment
    On some autumnal day,
And, dreaming like November,
    Find sleep without delay;
I, with my banners flying,
    I too must be away.

And when the gold bars, fading,
    Serene, august and still,
Lure me to cross their ramparts,
    Urged on by some strange will,
I shall know peace, and beauty,
    Beyond the last high hill.

An April Song

Now the jocund April comes—
    Hear her thin pipes playing!
How the world's white garden hums
With a million little drums!
    There is no delaying.

See the crocus lift its cup,
    Blue and golden yellow;
And the daffodils leap up,
Bidding us their wine to sup,
    Each a valiant fellow.

Gone the darkness! Now the dreams
    Of the flaming crocus.
Glad are we for rushing streams,
And the life that throbs and teems—
    Glad for spring that woke us.

Build, O April builders! Sing,
    Lest our frail hearts harden.
Once again the blossoms bring
Their sweet gospel with the spring—
    God is in His garden!

Kerry

I went back to Kerry—oh, after many years—
    Weary of the New World, longin' for the Old;
An' I saw the crooked streets, I saw them through tears,
    An' the little huddled houses against the sunset's gold.
Oh, Kerry town was a merry town when I was young;
    I minded me of all the lads an' all the girls I knew.
I minded me of all the songs that in my youth were sung,
    An' how above the chimney-pots the sky seemed always blue.
Kerry town, Kerry town, where my youth was spent;
Kerry town, the very town for old age and content.

I looked in many a doorway for faces I had known;
    I peeped in many a window, a-leanin' on me stick.
I well remembered every house an' every cobblestone,
    An' where, upon the mantleshelf, the tired clock would tick.
Oh, Kerry town was a fairy town when I was a lad;
    But now, how lonesome was the streets when I came back!
I thought the boys would welcome me, smile an' be glad;
    I'm growin' old and feeble, an' it's common sense I lack.

Kerry town, Kerry town, changed is every face;
Comin' back to Kerry town I find another place.

I'm changed meself. Yes, that I know—know it full well.
    The New World is on me though me old hair is white.
An' lads who were so simple would find it hard to tell
    That I was Michael Phelan, born in Kerry candlelight.
Oh, Kerry town's where I was born. I wanted it the same,
    But nothin' ever quite remains the way it used to be.
I'd rather the old friends was gone, for if I spoke me name
    An' they looked blank I think I'd weep that they'd
    forgotten me.
Kerry town, Kerry town, I'll kiss yer stones an' go,
For the New World, after all, is the only place I know.

Fugitive

The apple-blooms are out—
    How bright the world today!
My heart is like to shout
    Along the orchard way.
The lilac's perfumed buds are here—
This is the glory of the year.

What can I do but dream
    Of earth's transcendent face?
Here are the buds' pale cream
    On boughs that interlace,
And there I see the purple flowers
Illuminating May's white hours.

How brief these moments! Soon
    The light shall fade away,
And I be steeped in June
    On some enchanted day.
But now, my soul, look long and see
May's miracle on bush and tree.

Alone With Our Books

Sometimes, in the lamplight's glow,
When the world is shut from us, and even the delicate snow
Is a thing unknown,
We go to our shelves and take down our favorite books,
And in silence, with no inquiring looks,
Open them, and find ourselves in other worlds, alone.

O sweet and dear is this companionship!
We need no touch of hands, no press of lip,
Yet we are never so bound, so fast, so close, as when,
Locked from the world of men,
We two are thus alone—yet not alone—
Knowing a richness of life that only thus may be known.

Deep in your Æschylus, you read some tale
Of doom and fire; I, with Keats' nightingale,
Soar to a land of memory—to a vale
Red with the sun, or dim with the dawn's first light.
Lost, lost are we in valleys old and tired,
Or plunged in spiritual union with the dead.
Over your head,
Through the long silence of the night,
I see the nimbus of the flame outspread,

And I am happy in all I ever desired,
For I know, I know that the world, in these hours, is right.

I know that the tumult was worth it—to come to this;
To come to this rest of the soul,
With the lamp, like an aureole,
Burning in beauty above you,
(Ah! even that lamp doth love you!)
All that was fierce and wild in the years gone by;
All that was sad in our dread metropolis;
All the old terror I knew in days that are happily dead—
All, all that I lost makes these moments worth while,
Seeing your tears, and your smile,
Feeling the tempest within you surging once more
As you read, in this stillness, of passion and pain and war . . .
Yet between us no word has been said.

Only the voices of poets sing in our brain.
Vain, vain
Would be words of ours at such a time.
We are back in the world's lost prime,
And the present is like a false note, or a false rhyme.
We must pass back to the beginning of things,
On unseen wings;
We must hear the closing of Electra's door,
And the nightingale that sings, alas! no more.

Yet sometimes when I look
At you, O dearest, bending above your book
In the lamplight's glow,

I know
That you are lovelier than any poet's story.
You are my secret volume, touched with glory;
You are a history beyond the rough world's knowing,
And the strange riddle of you is forever flowing
Into my brain, into the core of my heart.
I have put you apart,
Like a dream for myself,
On some mysterious, inner, shining shelf;
And no one, as the moments rush and flee,
No one—save you and me—
No one shall ever know
Of this illuminated folio.

The Deathless Tale

I

Had He not breathed His breath
Truly at Nazareth;
Had not His very feet
Roamed many a hill and street;
Had Mary's story gone
To Time's oblivion;
Had the sweet record paled
And the truth not prevailed:
Dormant and bleak had been
This transitory scene,
And dark, thrice dark, our earth
Not knowing of His birth.

II

The flowers beheld His face,
The stars knew His white grace.
The grass was greener for
His humble stable door,
The rose upon its stem
Redder for Bethlehem.
And we—are we not wise

To cling with avid eyes
To the old tale and be
Moved by its memory?
Unutterably dim
Our bright world, lacking Him.

Slowly

There was no sudden moment when we said,
"Come! light the tapers—for our love is dead."

But gradually, through the slow and blundering years,
Unguessed of us, save for our casual tears,

Love wasted, like an invalid in a room,
Half hidden in the hushed and curtained gloom.

Prolonged that fluttering life, that ebbing breath.
And then, one day, dry-eyed we looked on Death;

And, since it came to us so unawares,
Frightened, we tiptoed down the darkened stairs.

Japanese Maidenhair Trees
(Bronx Park: Autumn)

I saw you, beautifully thinned,
    Like delicate, spun-gold candelabra
Touched by the autumn wind;
    And out of your stillness there came a voice
As of one who had never sinned.

How did you come, from the dust of the years,
    With your fragile, impermanent loveliness,
So close to our city of tears—
    So close to the panic and pain of Manhattan,
And close to its sorrow and fears?

O sweet! O more than heavenly sweet,
    You bless not only the border whereon you stand;
You bless for me now and forever each dingy street.
    You light, as with magical candles,
The paths of our dark city that eternally wait for my feet.

The Moon at the End of the Street

One night, strolling home in Manhattan,
    One wonderful night in July,
I saw, hanging over the Park,
Rising up out of the dark,
Clinging there, naked and stark,
    A torn yellow moon in the sky.

I thought: 'Tis a pot of wild honey
    That angels have overturned.
I watched it lean out of the night,
Golden and tawny and bright,
Put there for my lonely delight,
    A brass bowl tipped and burned.

And it poured its sweet honey over
    The aching and slumbering town.
Oh, bright the syrup that fell
On tower and citadel
In wonder no words can tell—
    A cascade rolling down.

Dear moon at the end of the street,
    Wild honey that sweetened the night,

You leaned with your old pity
Over the pavements gritty
Of the terrible sweltering city,
    And you filled my heart with your light.

Choice

I do not like late afternoon
    With shadows folding into dark.
Give me the morning with the tune
    Of the wild, happy meadowlark.
Give me the promise of the day,
    And the white glory of the sky,
With all the joy that these convey—
    A lover of the morning, I.

For morning hours are like white flowers,
    Opened, and drenched with dripping dew.
The honey of all heaven is theirs,
    Rich with earth's sweetness, too.
But shadows of late afternoon
    Cloud them with dim design.
Give me the morning's cup, filled up
    With beads of sun-stained wine.

A Charity Dance

After the dinner they had much enjoyed,
They gave a soirée for the unemployed.
The ladies rose with languor from their places,
A look of duty on their pretty faces.
The men, in tail-coats, moved like marionettes,
Puffing with unconcern their cigarettes.
In this warm, lavish room the fire leaped high,
Revealing figures on the tapestry,
And the rare paintings lining every wall.
Musicians placed themselves within the hall,
And soon the golden sounds rose to the ceiling.
Charity gives one such a pleasant feeling.
The dancers moved on light and airy feet.
(Outside, the Bread Line formed along the street.)

"I lost my shirt in Wall street," said a man,
Fresh from the South, with a rich coat of tan.
His linen was immaculate as wax.
Another said: "Oh, damn the income tax;
I've sold my holdings at a loss, and so
I won't pay any this year." "Really, Joe?
That's an idea. Let's have a drink up-stairs."
A while ago they both were millionaires,

But now they had a mere three millions left.
They thought that they were ruined and bereft.
"I've given up my yacht," a third one said,
Gulping his Scotch. "The market's worse than dead."
Each guest had paid ten dollars for this soirée.
(The poor outside? Oh, they were very sorry.)

The ladies paused and powdered their proud noses.
Lipsticks came out, redder than any roses.
"We're poor as churchmice," smiled a comely wife;
"I let the butler go—but that is life."
"I'm going to Paris soon—without my maid. . . .
My dear, where *did* you get that lovely jade?"
"Fred says we'll have to do with just one car.
Why, did you ever? But that's the way things are."
"I can't go to Bermuda with Jane Hallett,
And Harry has dismissed his negro valet."
"Things used to be so nice in this old town;
But servants' wages really *have* gone down!"
They moved away on light and nimble feet.
(Outside, the Bread Line shuffled down the street.)

On Receiving a Florist's Bill

Bittersweet, bayberries, hawthorn and roses—
These I must pay for before the month closes.
Coin of the realm shall be sent half a mile;
But how can you pay for a bayberry's smile?

And how can you pay for the scent of a rose,
Or the heart of white hawthorn? Ah! nobody knows.
Dull coin of the realm must be sent down the street
In exchange for the laughter of sweet bittersweet.

Blind in the City

All around him the city hummed:
    He could hear it, he could feel it—but he could not
        see;
And I thought, as his thin stick drummed
    On the agate flags, how must it seem and be
Thus to go on in the tumult of our town,
Wandering, wandering up and down.

Click-click! how his poor cane beat
    On the paves! How he moved, like a wraith. Yet he
        smiled;
And a few, in the fret of the street
    Paused to give aid—an old man, and a child.
But you and I, blinder than he, hurried on,
Started back. . . . But he was gone.

Six Little Ivory Elephants

There you are—seeming to move, yet never moving;
    Standing in a row upon my window-sill.
Out of the East you came mysteriously roving,
    But now you are still—so still.

Yet sometimes I think your bodies stumble
    And strain in your ivory line on my sill.
Often I think I hear you groan and grumble,
    And then I see you still—so still.

Ah! if you but knew it, there is sorrow—
    A jungle of darkness in the city beyond my sill.
Perhaps, like me, you will venture through it tomorrow,
    And then return—happy to be still.

When We Were Poor in Paris

When we were poor in Paris
    In everything save youth,
And the divine adventure,
    The magic quest of truth,
Life held a glorious vision
    Which riches cannot bring;
For I thought I was an artist,
    And you knew that you could sing.

When we were poor in Paris,
    (Ah! those were halcyon years,
With a crust a day for our *déjeuner*,
    And the solemn rent in arrears!)—
We laughed on the Champs Elysées
    In the soft blue afternoons,
And I told you of my pictures,
    You hummed your pretty tunes.

When we were poor in Paris
    The years were lean and long,
Yet Life was one bright Turner,
    And Love an old French song.
I daubed with crimson brushes,

  You trilled, and reached high *C;*
But no one bought my pictures—
  You only sang—for me.

Alas! those days have vanished,
  The shifter's changed the scene;
We're rich in wild Manhattan,
  And own our limousine.
But when the Maytime madness
  Comes swinging down the year,
O to be poor in Paris
  With you again, my dear!

Dead Tree

Stark against the sky
    A dead tree stands.
No bird sings in its boughs,
    No leaves are in its hands.
I see its ghostly shape
    Sharp before the sun.
It is an empty form,
    A sorry skeleton.

But in the jungle town,
    Against a marble wall
Yesterday I saw
    Something more horrible:
A living man, yet dead
    Like the bleak cypress tree,
A shadow of his self,
    A wraith of poverty.

And as the naked tree
    Had round it rich green things,
So this man stood gaunt,
    A beggar among kings.
Why had his leaves
    Vanished like the rose?
These are the things
    That no one knows.

Assunta's Rose

I

She used to water with her tears
    A single rose upon her sill;
And all the sisters smiled at her
    Within the convent on the hill.
"There is more beauty in a prayer
Than in a flower," they said to her.

Yet day by day she slipped away
    When vespers had been chanted low,
And bent above the fragrant bloom
    With tenderness that few may know.
Its incense floated to the skies,
Over the walls of paradise.

To her it seemed no wasted thing,
    Though she alone might love her flower.
The highway burned with sudden heat
    Far, far below her quiet tower,
And those who passed might never see
That rose in its red majesty.

And still the other sisters smiled,
    Then told their beads and bowed their heads;

They whispered that Assunta sinned,
    And prayed for her beside their beds.
"Earth's vanities!" they murmured. Yet
With her bright tears the rose was wet.

II

A troubadour went singing by
    When the green day was at its noon,
And the whole world was jubilant
    With the rich loveliness of June.
He passed the convent's heavy gate,
His heart enraptured and elate.

And as he gazed at silver clouds
    That floated high in heavenly seas,
And marveled at the miracle
    Of life, and earth's old sanctities,
He spied, within Assunta's jar,
The red rose shining like a star.

He never knew a brighter flower;
    He never saw a bloom more fair.
He crossed himself, and whispered, "Lord,
    Receive my humble, thankful prayer!"
And then he took his lute, and made
A song within the roadside shade.

III

The rose is gone. Assunta, too,
    Has left this world's defeat and pain.

The convent walls are ruins now,
    Kissed by long centuries of rain.
The troubadour has fled to God,
And all the nuns his path have trod.

But the glad song he made that day
    Goes ringing down the years! And men
Shall hear it till the stars are dust,
    And summer fails to smile again.
A deathless song, a deathless rose. . . .
I wonder if Assunta knows.

Old Dry-As-Dust

I

Old grey Dry-as-Dust—
    That's what we said o' him!
Pitiful old dullard—
    We had a sort o' dread o' him!
Always speakin' solemn things,
    Shakin' of his finger—
Around grey Dry-as-Dust
    No one long would linger.

"Thus—and—so," and "Mark—my—words,"
    "The young are scatterbrains!"—
These was the things he said—
    We all had better brains.
Foolish old Dry-as-Dust,
    Preachin' every minute
A long, long rigmarole—
    We saw nothin' in it.

"Do—*right!*" cried Dry-as-Dust;
    We laughed and winked at him.
"Virtue—*pays!*" he roared at us;
    We smiled an' blinked at him.

"Don't—be—foolish, lads!"
    "Keep away—from *evil!*"
We cried in a chorus then,
    "Go-to-the-devil!"

II

Long ago, Dry-as-Dust
    Died one Michaelmas.
Ed Boots married
    A foolish an' fickle lass.
Keith Dole wandered far
    Where the seas thunder.
The winds o' the world
    Blew us all asunder.

Hal Tuck's left his wife
    An' four poor kids he had.
God! the last year or two
    What thick red lids he had!
Everyone called him
    The young-boy drinker;
An' yet he might 'a' been
    A prosperous tinker.

I went downwards,
    Jus' like the rest o' them;
Couldn't keep straight
    On the path with the best o' them.
But the worst of us all
    Was poor Bill Parke

Who shot the gal he ruined—
    Shot her in the dark.

An' when I went to see him
    There in his prison place,
With his hands in gyves,
    An' a curious wizen' face,
What d'ye think he said
    When I came in?—
"Dry-as-dust was right, me lad!"
    In a voice high an' thin.

"Dry-as-Dust, he said it true—
    Laugh if ye will, me boy!
But I wisht I'd listened more—
    At least kep' still, me boy!"
God! how he looked at me—
    Poor Bill Parke,
Who went to the gallows
    Fer a foolish lark!

www.ingramcontent.com/pod-product-compliance
Lightning Source LLC
LaVergne TN
LVHW041550070426
835507LV00011B/1023